# Homes in Hot Places

**Alan James**

Lerner Publications Company
Minneapolis

All words printed in **bold** are explained in the glossary on page 30.

Cover illustration *Zulu children of South Africa outside their beehive-shaped home, which is well designed for keeping cool in a hot country.*

First published in the U.S. in 1989 by Lerner Publications Company.

Copyright © 1987 Wayland (Publishers) Ltd., Hove, East Sussex. First published 1987 by Wayland (Publishers) Ltd.

**Library of Congress Cataloging-in-Publication Data**

James, Alan, 1943-
  Homes in hot places.

  Bibliography: p.
  Includes index.
  Summary: Describes how homes are designed and built in hot climates.
    1. Architecture, Domestic — Arid regions — Juvenile literature. 2. Architecture, Tropical — Juvenile literature. 3. Vernacular architecture — Juvenile literature. | 1. Architecture, Domestic — Arid regions. 2. Architecture, Tropical. 3. Dwellings | I. Title.
NA7117.A74J36   1989       728'.0913       88-23107
ISBN 0-8225-2132-6 (lib.bdg.)

Printed in Italy by G. Canale & C.S.p.A., Turin
Bound in the United States of America

1  2  3  4  5  6  7  8  9  10  98  97  96  95  94  93  92  91  90  89

# Contents

What is a hot place?. . . . . . . . . 4

Homes in hot places. . . . . . . . . 6

Keeping cool. . . . . . . . . . . . . 8

Changes in temperature. . . . . . . 10

Using the sun. . . . . . . . . . . . 12

Building materials. . . . . . . . . 14

More building materials. . . . . . . 16

Building skills. . . . . . . . . . . . 18

Designs and space. . . . . . . . . . 20

Living habits. . . . . . . . . . . . 22

Family groups. . . . . . . . . . . .24

Traditions. . . . . . . . . . . . . 26

Comfort in the home. . . . . . . . 28

Glossary. . . . . . . . . . . . . . 30

Books to read. . . . . . . . . . . .31

Index. . . . . . . . . . . . . . . . 32

# What is a hot place?

The hot parts of the world are mostly to be found in a wide band around the **equator**. The equator is an imaginary line which runs in a circle around the middle of our planet. Hot countries often have **temperatures** higher than 86° Fahrenheit (30° Celsius), and sometimes as high as 122° F (50° C).

The weather of any place is the daily temperature, the wind, the rain, and the amount of sunshine. The usual kind of weather that a place has over a long period is called the **climate**. For example, a country may have hot summers and cooler winters.

There are different types of hot climates. Some places have a damp, **humid** heat; others have a dry heat. **Rain forests** are hot and steamy places where it rains heavily nearly every day. **Deserts** have a hot, dry heat. Many deserts are windy places, especially during the summer days.

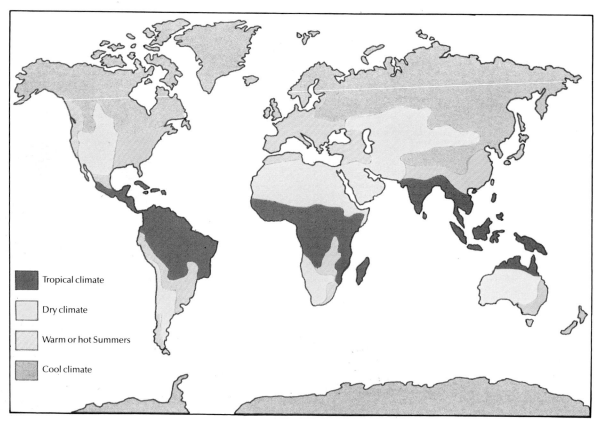

Tropical climate

Dry climate

Warm or hot Summers

Cool climate

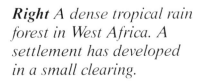

Hot places of the world include many countries in Africa, Australia, some Asian countries, and parts of South America. Several states in the southern U.S.A. (including Texas, California, and Florida) have very high temperatures. Some European countries, such as Spain, Greece, and Italy have very hot summers. Even some areas farther from the equator, such as New York State, can be very hot for part of the summer.

**Above** *The dry and barren landscape of the Sahara Desert, the world's largest desert*

**Left** *A map of the world showing the different types of climate*

**Right** *A dense tropical rain forest in West Africa. A settlement has developed in a small clearing.*

5

# Homes in hot places

We usually think of a house as having walls, a roof, rooms, doorways, floors, windows, electricity, and running water. But in many parts of the world, houses have only one or two of these features. Yet they are still comfortable places to live.

People may buy or build homes for many reasons. They want shelter from the weather. They want a familiar place to live during the day and somewhere to sleep at night. They want a private place where they feel safe and can keep all of their belongings.

A home in a hot country must provide shelter and shade from the fierce rays of the sun. People work out the best **design** and building materials to use, depending on the area where they live. Some houses in hot countries are very simple coverings, providing little more than temporary shelters from the heat of the sun. In fact, the word "shelter" simply means "something that is a barrier against heat, cold, and rain."

Other homes in hot places, built as permanent homes, have very thick walls to keep out the sun and make the house cool inside. As you will see, homes can look very different, but they all offer protection against the blazing heat of the sun.

*Left A shelter made from sticks and wire mesh, in the African bush, provides temporary protection from the sun.*

**Left** The sloping roofs of houses in Indonesia provide protection from the sun's rays, and allow heavy rains to drain away easily.

**Below** These flat-roofed houses in the desert have thick walls and tiny windows as protection from the sun's heat.

# Keeping cool

Some houses in places with very hot summers, such as Spain and Afghanistan, are built around an open-air courtyard. Windows of rooms look out onto this courtyard. This area is often used as an outdoor room where people work or just sit in a shady place. The air inside becomes cool at night and stays cool in the daytime, keeping rooms comfortable. These houses have only a few windows, and many have flat roofs. Sometimes people sleep on these roofs at night.

Houses in hot lands often have small windows and wooden window **shutters** to keep out the sun during the hottest part of the day, around noon. Builders may place a windtower—a tower which is designed to capture cool air and lead it to the lower floors—at the very top of a

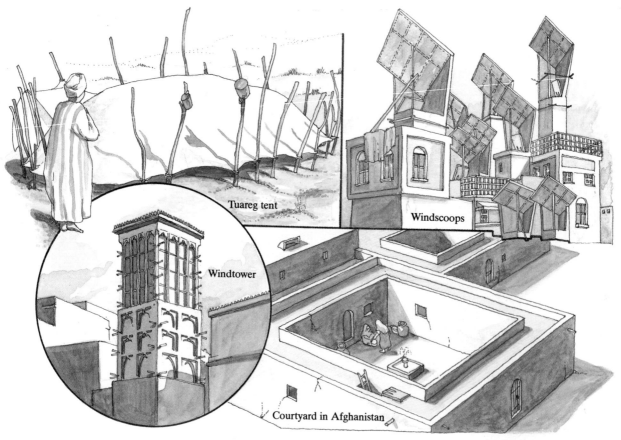

Tuareg tent

Windscoops

Windtower

Courtyard in Afghanistan

*Right* These adobe houses in the U.S.A. are made of clay, which can absorb heat during the day and then release it at night.

*Left* Four methods of reducing heat: the Tuareg tent can be rolled up to allow breezes to pass underneath; windscoops direct cooling breezes into the home; courtyards provide a shaded area; and windtowers allow winds to pass freely into buildings.

structure. Other types of houses may have large windows that are left open so that cooling breezes can blow through every room.

An **air-conditioning system** is put into some houses to keep rooms at a pleasant temperature. The air in a room can be changed and made warm or cool, moist or dry. Some of the hottest places on earth are in the deserts of Arizona. Many houses built there have been made of thick **adobe** bricks dried in the sun. This clay brick soaks up the sun's rays during the hottest part of the day—keeping the inside cool—and releases the stored heat during the night when the temperature falls a great deal.

The Tuareg tribes living in the Sahara Desert in Africa construct tents whose walls do not reach the ground, allowing breezes in.

In some places, including western Pakistan, large windscoops are placed on the roof to catch cool breezes and direct them down into the rooms below.

# Changes in temperature

When the hot sun goes down in the evening, the drop in temperature is immediate. People begin to feel much cooler quite soon afterwards.

In moist places, less heat from the sun reaches the ground during the day. This happens because water in the air acts like a filter for the sun's rays. Another result of moist air is that it will keep a place hot at night because heat is trapped close to the ground by the "water" filter.

Many deserts are dry for most or all of the year. This means that more hot rays reach the ground and the daytime temperatures are high. When the desert air is clear and dry, about 90 percent of the sun's rays reach the ground during the day. About the same amount of heat rises away from the surface of the desert through the clear, dry air at night. So during the night there are fairly low temperatures.

*Left* The climate in the jungle is hot and humid, with only a small difference between day and nighttime temperatures.

*Below* The Tuareg tribes-people, who live in tents in the Sahara Desert, often cook around an open fire.

In Algeria, in North Africa, the difference in temperature between day and night has been almost 54° F (30° C). In Libya (also in North Africa), an even more dramatic difference in temperature of 68° F (38° C) was recorded.

Houses must be built with thick materials that will keep people warm at night and keep the heat out during the day. **Nomads** living in tents need to light fires in the evening to keep themselves warm.

*Left* As the sun sets, heat rises from the ground, and the desert cools. Desert nights can be quite cold.

11

# Using the sun

In countries where there are long periods of sunshine, the **energy** from the sun can be used very successfully in the home for heating water or supplying electricity. A house with **solar** equipment on its roof collects light from the sun and converts it into heat energy. The flat, reflective part of the equipment is called a solar panel.

Solar panels are fixed on the outside of the roof on the side of the house that gets the most sunshine —facing south in the northern half of the world and facing north in the southern half. Some panels automatically turn to face the sun as the earth rotates.

Each panel is covered with glass, perhaps with double or triple **glazing**. Water runs in a pipe over the solar panel, underneath the glass, and is heated by the sun. The water flows by pipe to a solar water tank, where the heat is transferred to the water already there. When hot water is needed in the house, the water usually flows from the solar tank to the ordinary hot water tank and then to the faucet. Water is continually pumped through the system, from the roof back to the water tanks.

*Left The solar equipment on this roof collects light and heat from the sun and converts it into useful energy.*

*Right A solar home with solar panels. The sun heats the cold water that is pumped around the system of pipes in the solar panel.*

Cold water in

Glass

Sun's rays

Insulation

Black absorber plate

Pipes

Hot water out

Other solar panels can convert the heat from the sun into electricity. The power is stored in batteries and is used to provide electric power for the house.

13

# Building materials

Many materials can be used to build a house—stone, brick, concrete, mud, bamboo, wood, leaves, grass, woven wool, and animal skin. People often collect the building materials that are available to them in their country and which they can most easily use.

In parts of Africa, South America, and Asia, houses in villages often have a floor made of bamboo that is raised up on wooden **stilts**. This raised floor helps to keep animals out of the house and allows cooling breezes to blow beneath the house. The Quechua Indians of Peru, in South America, even have bamboo homes with open sides to let air in the house.

In Peru, many houses have large roofs covered with thick, large leaves to keep out the heavy rain. In places such as New Guinea, natural fibers including grass, banana leaves, or palm leaves are used to cover the roof. The walls are covered with matting, grass, or bamboo. A framework of young branches underneath gives the **structure** its shape.

The Kirdi tribespeople, who live in the grasslands in northern Cameroon (in central Africa), build

homes with leaves and grass placed on top of the roof to help absorb much of the heat from the sun. This keeps the house fairly cool inside.

Animals can provide building materials for homes. There are houses in East Africa built by the Masai people from cow dung. Hair from goats is woven into thick, waterproof material which can be made into tents by the Bedouin and other nomadic tribes.

14

**Left** This house in New Guinea is made of natural materials. It is raised on stilts, which helps keep animals out and prevents damage in case of flooding.

**Right** These mud houses in central Africa have thick, pointed roofs which absorb the heat of the sun.

**Below** These waterproof tents are woven from animal hair by nomadic tribes, such as the Bedouin.

# More building materials

Mud is cheap and easy to work and shape. It is often mixed with straw, to help harden it, and pressed into molds to form blocks. Some soils turn rock-hard in the sun.

Wood is often used to build homes, especially in dry places such as Australia or the southern states of the U.S.A. Natural wood rots quickly in wet places, so it must be painted or **varnished** to protect it from rain and hot sunshine. Window shutters made from wood keep out the strong rays of the sun.

Bricks, clay, stone, and concrete are all long-lasting building materials, used all over the world.

**Above** *The builder of this house in Cameroon uses mortar to hold the bricks together.*

**Left** *This house in Massachusetts has been painted and treated to withstand both heat and snow.*

**Right** *White paint on these buildings in Spain reflects the sun and protects the bricks.*

Bricks are made of clay mixed with small stones and other materials that strengthen them. Molded bricks are baked at a high temperature until very hard. **Mortar** holds them together to make a wall. Clay is also used to make tiles for roofs. Different clays have varying colors. Roofs in Spain are often made from red clay tiles.

Stone is cut in a **quarry** and is sometimes used to build the walls of a house. Often these walls are painted to protect them.

Concrete is increasingly used to build modern homes. It is made of small stones, called gravel, mixed with sand and cement. After water has been added to concrete, it sets hard in a few hours. Reinforced concrete has metal rods set inside it that make it even stronger. Concrete allows buildings to be made in new ways and in attractive shapes.

Metal can be used as the main material to build houses. Homes in **shantytowns** in India and South America are made of corrugated iron.

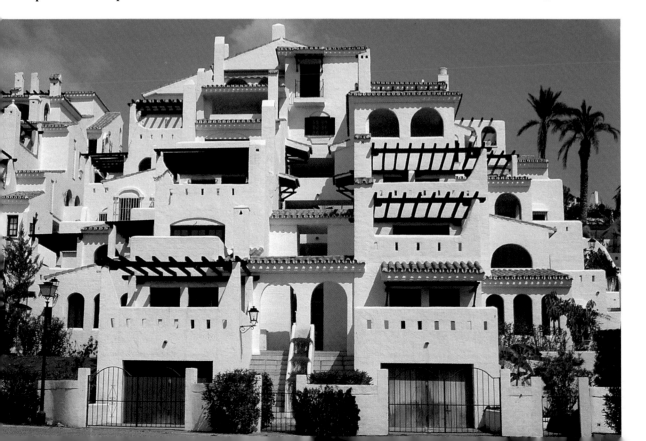

# Building skills

The kinds of houses people construct depend partly on how skillful they are at building shelters. Using the most limited materials, people have developed skills for building wonderfully effective temporary homes. With more materials available, they might make a large, permanent home with more than one **story**.

Bushmen living in the Kalahari Desert (in the southwest part of Africa) often move about hunting for animals. These nomads build temporary homes at their campsites beside water holes. Each family has its own simple shelter called a **skerm**. Skerms are made with a frame of slender branches and covered with long grasses. The women of the tribe usually build these shelters.

Traditional homes in west Kenya are made with mud. A wooden frame is filled with wet mud, which is then left in the sun to bake hard. The roof is then **thatched**. In Saudi Arabia, there are more complex mud houses up to four stories high.

In all parts of the world, and especially in cities, highly developed building skills are being applied. Expert builders are able to use modern materials and new knowledge, as well as machinery, to construct large, complex houses. These modern structures often rise many stories and are designed to provide comfort whatever the climate.

**Left** *Thatching the roof of a baked mud house in Niger*

18

**Left** *On this building site in Singapore, cranes and heavy machinery are used to move building materials.*

**Below** *A view of Saudia Arabia's capital city, Riyadh, showing the variety in design of concrete buildings*

# Design and space

People in hot places have to plan carefully the way their home is laid out (its design) to protect themselves from overpowering heat, winds, and sometimes heavy rainfall. The home's design can also depend on what people can afford—the poor live in simple houses, while the wealthy live in homes with many rooms. Streets can be designed, too. Towns in Saudi Arabia and Spain, for instance, have many homes crowded fairly close together in narrow streets. The houses shade each other from the sun.

Some people today even live in caves—just as people did thousands of years ago. They use the natural layout of the caves, sometimes altering a cave to make it larger. Today, Gypsies live in caves on the hillsides of Granada in the south of Spain. In Tunisia, North Africa, there are many caves and even underground homes at Matmata. These homes are hollowed out of soft rock and furnished comfortably. Underground, people keep cool, find water, and take shelter from the winds. In Coober Pedy, Australia, some people live in abandoned mining tunnels.

Homes in hot places are often circular in shape, sometimes with no windows. This means that as little as possible of the outer surface is exposed to the midday sun. Many homes in Syria are beehive-shaped, and some homes in Greece have curved roofs for this reason. Larger, more complex houses usually have rooms that are square or rectangular.

**Left** *These houses in Cordoba, in Spain, are built closely together in narrow streets to shade one another from the sun.*

_**Left** These Gypsy cave dwellings in Granada, Spain, are hollowed out of soft rock and provide a cool home underground._

_**Below** A beehive-shape lessens a house's exposure to the sun, as the sun's strongest rays can only reach a small surface area._

In general, the larger the house, the more difficult it is to cool and heat it.

Apartment buildings in many hot countries are designed with air-conditioning systems and also **balconies** where people can dry washing, sit in the sunshine, or enjoy the cool evening air.

21

# Living habits

Some people never leave the village or town where they were born. They might even live in the same house for their entire lives. Others move from one house to another after a few years, perhaps when they go to a new place to get a different job or when their family grows and they need a bigger house. But all of these people live settled lives in permanent homes—in towns, in villages, or in farmhouses. Their homes can be made of bricks, stones, sheets of metal, clay, or heavy wood.

*Right* People who live in hot areas near a desert, like this family in Australia, may experience chilly evenings. Outdoor activities go on despite the change in temperature.

*Left* These nomads, who are wandering travelers without permanent homes, carry their possessions on the back of a camel.

Other people, such as nomads, regularly travel from one place to another, looking for water holes and new pastureland for their animals. Perhaps every week or two they move to another campsite.

Nomads need shelters that are lightweight and can be easily moved. The shelters must also be small enough to carry. Most nomads have tent homes. A nomad tent can be put up and possessions arranged inside it in less than two hours.

In many hot countries, various activities such as washing, cooking on a **barbecue**, and relaxing are done in public. Many people only return to their separate homes to sleep.

Because of the intense heat of the noon sun in some hot countries like Italy, Greece, and Spain, people go to work early and then relax or sleep for two or more hours around midday. They then work into the evening and eat dinner quite late. The time they take off in the afternoon is called a **siesta**.

# Family groups

The size of house a family owns depends partly on what they can afford to buy or build. It also depends on how many people will be living in the house. Around the world, homes can be designed very differently. They may be suitable for one or a number of people, perhaps settled in family groups. In some places, the size of the family can be quite large, so the building needs to be quite big.

In some countries, almost the whole village might live in a large "family" group inside one **longhouse**. Relatives, friends, young and old all live together. They even sleep in the one huge room, perhaps using different parts of the floor as their own special area. In Sarawak, in Malaysia, there are longhouses on stilts. Each family has a separate room. New rooms are added as more people come. The Dayak people of Borneo also have this kind of home. The Cherokee Indians, who once controlled the northeastern United States, traditionally lived in longhouses as well.

In northern Ghana, the Nabdan tribe lives in family units. Each family owns a group of round mud homes, joined together by walls.

When sons marry, new rooms are added for their wives.

So the size of a "family" depends on the usual way people group themselves in a certain place. How they are grouped depends on the customs, habits, and ways of life found in their part of the world.

*Below In some countries, like the U.S.A., the word "family" usually includes only parents and their young children.*

**Above** Each family lives in a separate room in a Dayak home in Borneo.

**Right** A family outside their home in Nairobi, Kenya

# Traditions

People can choose to build their houses with any number of rooms. Houses can be built to stand alone, on opposite sides of a street, or around the sides of a central square. Some are built in a pattern that has a meaning. The Dogon houses in Mali, Africa, are built in a special way. The layout of a village's houses, towers, storerooms, goat houses, passages, shrine, and stables represents the parts of the human body.

In some parts of the world, a circular building is thought to be lucky or even holy. In parts of China, the way a house should face may be predicted by a fortune-teller.

Traditional houses in Australia and the southern United States often have **verandahs** outside, where people can relax in the cool breezes of the evening.

The large tent used by nomads in Morocco is of similar design to the

homes in Timbuktu, Mali, which use bamboo frames that are covered with skins. Timbuktu was founded long ago by nomads from the Sahara Desert, and so the traditional designs spread from one area to another.

A Bedouin tent has curtains inside. Bedouins divide up the space so there are separate areas for different activities such as cooking or entertaining visitors. But the traditional tent-dwelling existence of the Bedouin is slowly changing. Many Bedouin people now lead settled lives in permanent homes.

It is usually possible to tell whether a house is from Mali, Italy, or the U.S.A., for instance, because different countries often have distinctive national designs, patterns, and materials.

*Left* A traditional country home in Australia, with a verandah and corrugated iron roof

*Left* The layout of a Dogon township in Mali

*Right* Bedouin children, who have resettled in a permanent concrete home, play in the sand.

# Comfort in the home

Standards of comfort in a home change very much from country to country, people to people. In hot places, some people have very simple homes and few belongings, while other people have many possessions in their homes.

Often houses in hot places do not have carpets. Many have attractive floor tiles instead. These are easy to keep clean and cool to walk on. People in hot places need no blankets on their beds for much of the year. The Yanomamo Indians of Brazil sleep without bedding in hammocks suspended from the roofs of their homes.

Many homes have an electric fan which helps to blow cool air around the rooms. Shrubs and trees outside the building help shade it from the sun and make it cooler.

**Architects** and others who design houses often think of homes as machines for living in, meaning that homes must be suited to the needs of daily life. They are places where people eat, sleep, store their possessions and so on. A house is a machine that must be designed and built to a sensible plan if it is to be used efficiently for all of these things.

But a home is much more than a machine. It is a very personal place —usually a special place for a particular family. No two homes ever look exactly alike inside even if they look alike in their outside design. Each piece of furniture or decoration makes a house reflect the owner's personality.

28

**Left** Homes in Sydney, Australia, with greenery on the roof to help absorb the heat

**Right** This Turkish family has an electric fan moving the air to keep their home comfortable.

**Below** A thatched house in Micronesia. Many possessions are made of natural materials.

# Glossary

**adobe** Brick that has been dried and hardened by the sun

**air-conditioning system** System in a building which raises or lowers the temperature of the air, or makes it drier or damper

**architect** A person who designs buildings

**balcony** A place to sit in the open air outside an upstairs room

**barbecue** Food cooked over a fire or coals; cooking and eating in the open

**climate** The usual weather of a place over a very long period

**desert** A dry, barren area, usually mostly sand

**design** A pattern or plan of a building

**energy** The ability to do work, such as to increase temperature; power, such as electricity, that can be used to do work

**equator** An imaginary line around the earth half-way between the North and South poles

**glazing** A method of treating glass to make it stronger and harder for heat to escape through

**humid** Having moist, damp air

**longhouse** A long, large house shared by many people

**mortar** A mixture of sand, lime, and water used for fixing bricks or stones together

**nomad** A person with no permanent home who travels in search of pasture for his or her animals

**quarry** A place where stone is removed from the ground

**rain forest** A forest which grows near the equator where there is heavy rainfall all year. Rain forests are very hot and steamy.

**rotate** To turn around like a wheel

**shantytown** A town or slum made up of crude dwellings, often made using waste pieces of wood or corrugated iron. Shantytowns are usually very crowded, with houses close together.

**shutters** Movable wooden covers for the outside of the window

**siesta** An afternoon rest period observed in many hot countries

**skerm** A shelter built by the Kalahari Bushmen of Africa, made of slender branches and long grass

**solar** Relating to the sun; produced or operated by the sun's light or heat

**stilts** Wooden poles on which a house stands above the ground

**story** A level or floor of a house or building

**structure** The frame on which the covering of a building is laid

**temperature** The amount of heat in a place or thing

**thatched** A roof covered with reeds, straw, or leaves

**varnished** Painted with a solution to give it a shiny, hard surface

**verandah** Partly open section on the outside of a house usually covered by the main roof; a large porch

# Books to read

*A Place in the Sun* by Lois and Louis Darling (William Morrow and Company, 1968).
*American Indians Today* by Olga Hoyt (Abelard-Schuman, 1972).
*A World Full of Homes* by William A. Burns (McGraw-Hill Book Company, 1953).
*Houses Around the World* by Louise and Richard Floethe (Charles Scribner's Sons, 1973).
*Sons of the Desert* by Sonia and Tim Gidal (Pantheon Books, 1960).

---

### Houses and Homes

Building Homes                    Homes in Space
Castles and Mansions              Homes in the Future
Homes in Cold Places             Homes on Water
Homes in Hot Places              Mobile Homes

---

## Picture Acknowledgements

The author and publishers would like to thank the following for the illustrations in this book: Bryan and Cherry Alexander, p. 9; David Bowden Photographic Library, p. 28; Bruce Coleman Ltd., p. 29; Chris Fairclough, p. 23; Jimmy Holmes, p. 10; Alan Hutchison, pp. 6, 11 (bottom), 16 (top), 18, 26; Christine Osborne Pictures, pp. 7 (bottom), 17, 22, 27 (top and bottom); Shell Photo Service, p. 12; ZEFA, pp. 5 (top and bottom), 7 (top), 11 (top), 14, 15 (top and bottom), 16 (bottom), 19 (bottom), 21 (top and bottom). All other pictures from the Wayland Picture Library. Bruce Coleman, *cover.*

# Index

Numbers in **bold** refer to
illustrations.

adobe houses, 9, **9**
Afghanistan, 8
Africa, 5, **5**, **6**, 11, 14, **15**,
    18, 20
air-conditioning, 9, 21
Algeria, 11
animals, 14, 18, 23
architects, 28
Asia, 14
Australia, 5, 16, 20, **23**, 26,
    **27**, **28**

balconies, 21
bamboo houses, 14, 27
Bedouin tribe, 14, **15**, 27,
    **27**
Borneo, 24, **25**
bricks, 16, 17
Bushmen, 18

Cameroon, 14, **16**
caves, 20, **21**
circular houses, 20, **21**,
    26
concrete houses, 17
courtyards, **8**

Dayak homes, **25**
Dayak people, 24
deserts, 4, **7**, 9, 10, **10**, 27
Dogon houses, 26, **27**

electric fan, 28, **28**
equator, 4

Ghana, 24
Greece, 20, 23
Gypsies, 20

India, 5, 17
Indonesia, **7**
Italy, 5, 23

Kalahari Desert, 18
Kenya, 18, **25**
Kirdi houses, **15**
Kirdi tribe, 14

Libya, 11

Malaysia, 24
Mali, 26
Masai people, 14
metal houses, 17
Micronesia, **28**
Morocco, 26
mud buildings, 18

Nabdan tribe, 24
New Guinea, 14, **14**
Niger, **18**
nomads, 11, 18, 23, **23**, 27

Peru, **11**, 14, 24, 28

rain forests, 4, **5**
roofs, 8, 12, 14, 27

Sahara Desert, **5**, **11**, 27
Saudi Arabia, 18, **19**, 20
shantytowns, 17
shutters, 8, 16
skerms, 18
Singapore, **19**
solar home, **13**
solar panels, 12, **12**, 13
South America, 14
Spain, 5, 8, 20, **20**, **21**, 23
stilts, 14, **14**, 24
Syria, 20

tents, 9, 11, **11**, **15**, 23
Tuareg tent, **8**
Tuareg tribe, 9, **11**
Tunisia, 20

U.S.A., 5, 9, **16**, **24**, 26

verandah, 26, **27**

water holes, 18, 23
water vapor, 10
windows, 6, **8**, 16
windscoops, **8**, 9
windtowers, 8, **8**
wooden houses, 16

Quechua Indians, 14

Yanomamo Indians, 28